To:

From:

Published by Sourcebooks, Inc.
P.O. Box 4410, Naperville, Illinois 60567-4410
(630) 961-3900
FAX: (630) 961-2168
www.sourcebooks.com

ISBN 1-57071-998-5

Printed and bound in Thailand
IM 10 9 8 7 6 5 4 3 2 1

KISS ME
You Fool

SOURCEBOOKS CASABLANCA™
AN IMPRINT OF SOURCEBOOKS, INC.®
NAPERVILLE, ILLINOIS

I can resist everything except

TEMPTATION.

—*Oscar Wilde*

The pleasure of L O V E is in loving. We are happier in the P A S S I O N we feel than in that we arouse.

—*François, Duc de La Rochefoucauld*

L O V E sought is good,

but giv'n unsought is better.

—*William Shakespeare*

I clasp thy waist;

I feel thy bosom's beat.

O, K I S S me into faintness,

sweet and dim.

—*Alexander Smith*

She gave me a S M I L E

I could feel in my hip pocket.

—*Raymond Chandler*

Give all to L O V E ;

obey thy H E A R T .

—*Ralph Waldo Emerson*

kiss me

Only he felt he could no more dissemble,

and K I S S E D her, mouth to mouth,

all in a tremble.

—*Leigh Hunt*

At the

TOUCH

of love everyone

becomes a

POET.

—*Plato*

So sweet LOVE seemed that April morn,

When first we KISSED beside the thorn,

So strangely SWEET, it was not strange

We thought that LOVE could never change.

—Robert Bridges

Love alters not with T I M E' S brief hours and weeks, but bears it out even to the edge of doom.

—William Shakespeare

Bring me my bow
of burning gold, Bring
me my arrows of
D E S I R E, Bring
me my spear O clouds,
unfold! Bring me my
chariot of F I R E!

—*William Blake*

And stood we by the rose-wreathed gate. Alas,

We L O V E D , sir—used to meet:

How sad and bad and mad it was—

But then, how it was

S W E E T !

—*Robert Browning*

I wrote the story myself. It's all about a girl who lost her reputation but never missed it.

—*Mae West*

You must

remember this,

a K I S S is still a kiss.

—*Herman Hupfeld*

When you K I S S me,

jaguars lope through my knees;

when you K I S S me, my lips

quiver like bronze violets;

oh, when you K I S S me.

—*Diane Ackerman*

LOVE is the answer, but while you are waiting for the answer, sex raises some pretty good questions.

—*Woody Allen*

I don't care what people do, as long as they don't do it in the street and frighten the horses.

—*Mrs. Patrick Campbell*

That which we call sin in

others is experiment for us.

—*Ralph Waldo Emerson*

A K I S S can be a comma, a question mark, or an exclamation point. That's basic spelling that every woman ought to know.

—*Mistinguett (Jeanne Marie Bourgeois)*

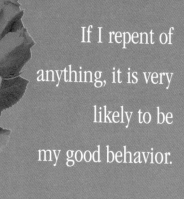

If I repent of anything, it is very likely to be my good behavior.

—*Henry David Thoreau*

One must not lose

DESIRES.

They are mighty stimulants

to creativeness, to love,

and to long life.

—*Alexander Bogomoletz*

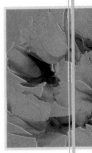

For flavor, instant sex will never supersede the stuff you have to peel and cook.

—Quentin Crisp

You never know what is
enough, until you know what
is more than enough.

—*William Blake*

All human
activity is
prompted by
DESIRE.

—*Bertrand Russell*

There are some days

when I think I'm going to

die from an overdose of

SATISFACTION.

—*Salvador Dali*

kiss me

She lifted her D E L I C A T E,
high-bred face, F E A R L E S S love
S H I N I N G in every lineament, to his,
and they exchanged their first K I S S.

—*Lucy Maud Montgomery*

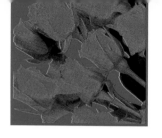

The essential
conditions of
everything you
do must be
choice, love,
PASSION.

—*Nadia Boulanger*

When a woman unhappily yoked talks about the S O U L with a man not her husband, it isn't the soul they are talking about.

—*Don Marquis*

43

Take away all from me,

but leave me E C S T A S Y,

and I am richer than all my fellow men.

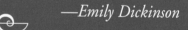

—*Emily Dickinson*

In B L I S S these
creatures are born,
in B L I S S they are
sustained, and
to B L I S S they
merge again.

—The Vedas

Follow your D E S I R E as long as you live…When riches are gained, follow D E S I R E, for riches will not profit if one is sluggish.

—Ptahhotep

kiss

Sex is like having dinner; sometimes you joke about the dishes, sometimes you take the meal seriously.

—*Woody Allen*

The S O U L should always stand ajar,

ready to welcome the ecstatic experience.

—Emily Dickinson

Give me a KISS
TO build a
DREAM on and
my imagination will
thrive upon that
KISS.

—*Louis Armstrong*

I'm going to give you only one lip when we K I S S . Because if I give you two, you'll never live through it.

—*Woody Allen*

I am certain of nothing but of
the holiness of the
H E A R T ' S affections, and
the truth of the
I M A G I N A T I O N .

—John Keats

The act of

LONGING

for something will

always be more

intense than the

REQUITING

of it.

—*Gail Godwin*

First time he K I S S E D me,

    he but only kissed

The fingers of this hand wherewith I write;

And, ever since, it grew more

    clean and white.

—Elizabeth Barrett Browning

You learn LOVE by loving—by paying attention and doing what one thereby DISCOVERS has to be done.

—Aldous Huxley

The prerequisite for
making L O V E is to like
someone enormously.

—*Helen Gurley Brown*

One word frees us of all the
weight and pain of life: that
word is L O V E.

—*Sophocles*

Brevity is the
S O U L of
lingerie.

—*Dorothy Parker*

When you come to be sensibly touched, the scales will fall from your E Y E S ; and by the penetrating eyes of love you will discern that which your other eyes will never S E E .

—*François de la Mothe Fénelon*

Platonic friendship is the interval

between the introduction and

the FIRST KISS.

—*R. Woods*

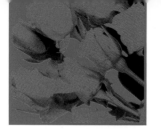

The capacity for

PASSION

is both cruel and

DIVINE.

—*George Sand*

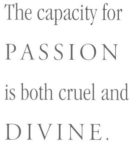

66

The average Hollywood film star's ambition is to be admired by an American, courted by an Italian, married to an Englishman, and have a French boyfriend.

—*Katharine Hepburn*

The only sin PASSION can

commit is to be joyless.

—*Dorothy L. Sayers*

The best way to

H O L D a man

is in your arms.

—*Mae West*

Compared to my heart's D E S I R E

the sea is a drop.

—*Adélia Prado*

kiss

DESIRE

can blind us to

the hazards of

our enterprises.

—*Marie de France*

71

I kissed my first W O M A N and smoked my first cigarette on the same day. I have never had time for tobacco since.

—*Arturo Toscanini*

She K I S S E D as thirstily as ever, cupping her man's head in both hands and seeming very nearly to D R I N K from it.

—*Kenneth Tynan (on Greta Garbo)*

Let us now bask under the spreading trees said Bernard in a PASSIONATE tone. Oh yes lets said Ethel and she opened her dainty parasole and sank down upon the long grass. She closed her eyes but was far from asleep.

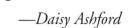

—*Daisy Ashford*

Love—bittersweet, irrepressible—

loosens my limbs and I tremble.

—*Sappho (6th century B.C.)*

It is impossible

to repent of love.

The sin of love

does not exist.

—*Muriel Spark*

O! a K I S S

Long as my exile, sweet as my revenge!

—*William Shakespeare*

Whatever our
S O U L S are
made of, his and
mine are the
S A M E .

—*Emily Brontë*

If I had never met him

I would have

DREAMED him

into being.

—*Anzia Yezierska*

LOVE is the only thing
that keeps me sane.

—*Sue Townsend*

Intense L O V E is often

akin to intense suffering.

—*Frances Ellen Watkins Harper*

I don't want to

L I V E —I want to

L O V E first, and

live incidentally.

—*Zelda Fitzgerald*

kiss me

here is the secret that's keeping the stars apart:

i carry your heart (i carry it in my heart)

—*e. e. cummings*

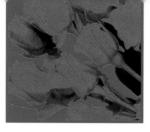

Whoever has loved

knows all that

L I F E contains

of sorrow and

of J O Y.

—George Sand

We LOVE because

it's the only true

ADVENTURE.

—*Nikki Giovanni*

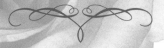

Great loves too must be E N D U R E D .

—*Coco Chanel*

Honor the

OCEAN

of love

—*George de Bennville*

It was the kind of desperate, headlong,

adolescent calf love that he should have

experienced years ago

and got over.

—*Agatha Christie*

kiss

I was in L O V E
with the whole
world and all that
lived in its rainy
arms.

—*Louise Erdrich*

95

KISSES are like grains of gold

or silver found upon the ground, of

no value themselves, but precious as

showing that a mine is NEAR.

—*George Villiers*

I was like twelve or something, when you first K I S S a guy and you see the way the guy reacts, how they get really excited, or whatever. And I'm perceptive, so I think, "Ah, jeez, is that something that I'm able to do?"

—*Juliette Lewis*

Awake, O north wind; and come, thou south; blow upon my garden, that the spices thereof may flow out. Let my B E L O V E D come into his garden, and eat his pleasant fruits.

—*Song of Solomon*

We L O V E what we should
scorn if we were W I S E R.

—*Marie de France*

The fate of L O V E is
that it always seems too
little or too much.

—*Amelia E. Barr*

The dictionary says that a K I S S is "a salute made by touching with the lips pressed closely together and suddenly parting them." From this it is quite obvious that, although a dictionary may know something about words, it knows nothing about K I S S I N G .

—*Hugh Morris*

I DREAM

that love

without tyranny

is possible.

—Andrea Dworkin

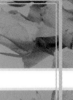
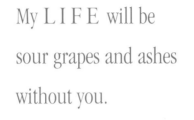

My L I F E will be

sour grapes and ashes

without you.

—*Daisy Ashford*

You need someone to

L O V E you while you're

looking for someone to

L O V E.

—*Shelagh Delaney*

Most of us LOVE from our need to LOVE, not because we find someone deserving.

—*Nikki Giovanni*

Till it has

LOVED, no

man or woman

can become itself.

—*Emily Dickinson*

LOVE is like the measles. The older you get it, the worse the ATTACK.

—Mary Roberts Rinehart

kiss me

"KISS" rhymes to "BLISS"

in fact as well as verse.

—*George Noel Gordon, Lord Byron*

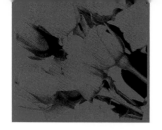

LOVE opens the doors into everything, as far as I can see, including and perhaps most of all, the door into one's own SECRET, and often terrible and frightening, REAL SELF.

—May Sarton

In a great R O M A N C E, each person basically plays a part that the other really likes.

—*Elizabeth Ashley*

It is better to know as
little as possible of the
defects of the person
with whom you are to
pass your L I F E.

—*Jane Austen*

The A B S O L U T E yearning of one
human body for another particular one
and its indifference to substitutes is one
of life's major mysteries.

—*Iris Murdoch*

Life is a

FLOWER

of which love is the

HONEY.

—*Victor Hugo*

kiss

119

I truly feel that there are as many ways of
L O V I N G as there are people in the
world and as there are days in the lives of
those people.

—*Mary S. Calderone*

I ducked my head in time, so that he was only able to imprint a chaste salute upon my forehead, as he pressed me against himself in a way I felt quite sure was not the custom of the country, at least only in as much as it is the custom of all countries.

—*Margaret Fountaine*

A man had given all other BLISS,

And all his worldly worth for THIS,

To waste his whole heart in one KISS

Upon her PERFECT LIPS.

—*Alfred, Lord Tennyson*

Human T H I R S T S are satisfied from time to time, but the thirst of the human skin is never S A T I S F I E D so long as it lives.

—*Joyce Carol Oates*

Men always want to be a woman's first love—women like to be a man's last romance.

—*Oscar Wilde*

When her loose gown from her
  shoulders did fall,
And she caught me in her arms
  long and small,
Therewith all sweetly did me
  KISS,
And softly said, "Dear heart, how like
  you this?"

—*Thomas Wyatt*

Gin a body meet a body

Coming through the rye;

Gin a body kiss a body,

Need a body cry?

—Robert Burns

There's plenty of F I R E

in the coldest flint!

—*Rachel Field*

How much B E T T E R

is thy love than wine!

—*Song of Solomon*

Cherry ripe, ripe, ripe, I cry,

Full and fair ones; come and buy!

If so be you ask me where

They do grow, I answer, there,

Where my Julia's lips do smile;

There's the land, or cherry-isle.

—*Robert Herrick*

The decision to K I S S for the first time is the most crucial in any love story. It changes the R E L A T I O N S H I P of two people much more strongly than even the final surrender; because this kiss already has within it that S U R R E N D E R.

—*Emil Ludwig*

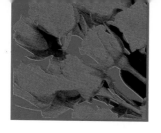

Nobody has ever
measured, even
poets, how much
a H E A R T
can hold.

—*Zelda Fitzgerald*

Come live with me, and be my love,

And we will some new pleasures prove

Of golden sands, and crystal brooks,

With silken lines, and silver hooks.

—*John Donne*

Love's mysteries in S O U L S do grow,

But yet the body is his book.

—*John Donne*

So true a fool is
L O V E that in
your will, though
you do anything,
he thinks no ill.

—*William Shakespeare*

The human H E A R T , at whatever age, opens only to the H E A R T that opens in return.

—*Maria Edgeworth*

At the

TOUCH

of love, everyone

becomes a

POET.

—*Plato*

kiss

This month is a K I S S

Which heaven gives the earth

That she now become a bride

And then a future mother.

—*Friedrich von Logau*

What is L O V E ? 'Tis not hereafter;

Present mirth hath present laughter.

What's to come is still unsure:

In delay there lies no plenty;

Then come K I S S me, sweet and twenty,

Youth's a stuff will not endure.

—*William Shakespeare*

A man when he is making up to anybody can be cordial and gallant and full of little attentions and altogether charming. But when a man is really I N L O V E he can't help looking like a sheep.

—*Agatha Christie*

Lovers who L O V E truly do not

write down their H A P P I N E S S .

—*Anatole France*

A PLEASURE so exquisite as almost to amount to PAIN.

—*Leigh Hunt*

Pity me that the H E A R T

is slow to learn

What the swift M I N D

beholds at every turn.

—*Edna St. Vincent Millay*

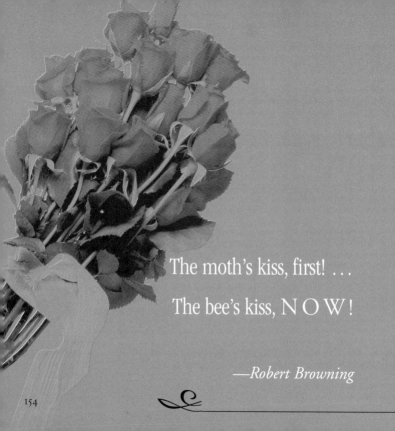

The moth's kiss, first! . . .

The bee's kiss, N O W !

—*Robert Browning*

BREATHLESS, we

flung us on the windy hill,

Laughed in the sun, and

KISSED the lovely grass.

—*Rupert Brooke*

Oh, thou art F A I R E R than

the evening air

Clad in the B E A U T Y of a

thousand stars.

—*Christopher Marlowe*

Thus I PACIFIED
Psyche and kissed her,
And TEMPTED her
out of her gloom.

—*Edgar Allan Poe*

Touch is the

LANDSCAPE

of what is

POSSIBLE.

—*Kate Green*

In her first P A S S I O N

woman loves her lover,

In all the others, all she loves

is L O V E .

—*George Noel Gordon, Lord Byron*

kiss me

Suns may set and rise again: for us,
when our brief light has set, there's the
sleep of perpetual night. Give me
A THOUSAND KISSES.

—*Gaius Valerius Catullus*

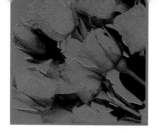

O Polly, you
might have
toyed and
K I S S E D,
By keeping men
off, you keep
them on.

—*John Gay*

His mouth is most S W E E T :
yea, he is altogether lovely. This
is my B E L O V E D, and this
is my friend.

—*Song of Solomon*

Pleasure's a S I N , and

sometimes sin's a P L E A S U R E.

—*George Noel Gordon, Lord Byron*

To be in L O V E is

to surpass oneself.

—*Oscar Wilde*

KISSING your hand may make
you feel very, very good, but a diamond
and sapphire bracelet lasts forever.

—*Anita Loos*

KISS ME,
Kate, we
will be married
o' Sunday.

—*William Shakespeare*

The red R O S E whispers of passion

And the white R O S E breathes of love;

O, the red R O S E is a falcon,

And the white R O S E is a dove.

—*John Boyle O'Reilly*

Be plain in dress, and sober in
your diet;
In short, my deary, K I S S M E,
and be quiet.

—*Lady Mary Wortley Montagu*

She [Aphrodite] spoke and loosened from her bosom the embroidered girdle of many colors into which all her allurements were fashioned. In it was love and in it desire and in it blandishing persuasion which steals the mind even of the wise.

—*Homer*

Here are fruits, flowers, leaves, and
branches,
And here is my H E A R T which
beats only for you.

—*Paul Verlaine*

Marriages are made in

HEAVEN and

consummated on Earth.

—*John Lyly*

O love, thy K I S S would wake the dead!

—*Alfred, Lord Tennyson*

Mademoiselle from

Armenteers,

Hasn't been kissed in

forty years.

— *"Red" Rowley*

Many waters cannot quench

L O V E , neither can the

floods drown it.

—*Song of Solomon*

Age does not protect you from

L O V E but love to some

extent protects you from age.

—*Jeanne Moreau*

LOVE is a

never ending feeling.

—*Adeil Prince*

The KISS you take is better than you give.

—*William Shakespeare*

kiss me

Jenny kissed me when we met,

Jumping from the chair she sat in;

Time, you thief, who love to get

Sweets into your list, put that in:

Say I'm weary, say I'm sad,

Say that health and wealth have missed me,

Say I'm growing old, but add,

JENNY KISSED ME.

—*Leigh Hunt*

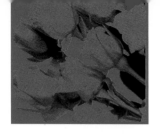

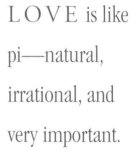

L O V E is like
pi—natural,
irrational, and
very important.

—Lisa Hoffman

And our lips found ways of

SPEAKING

What words cannot say,

Till a hundred nests gave music,

And the East was gray.

—*Frederick Lawrence Knowles*

KISS till the cow comes home.

—Francis Beaumont and John Fletcher

To L O V E and be
loved is to feel the sun
from both sides.

—*David Viscott*

When you L O V E someone,

all your saved-up W I S H E S

start coming out.

—*Elizabeth Bowen*

Came but for

FRIENDSHIP,

and took away love.

—*Thomas Moore*

kiss

Love is friendship

set on F I R E.

—*Jeremy Taylor*

Ae fond K I S S , and then we sever;

Ae farewell and then F O R E V E R !

—*Robert Burns*

Marriage is not a ritual or an end. It is a long, intricate, I N T I M A T E dance together and nothing matters more than your own sense of balance and your choice of P A R T N E R.

—*Amy Bloom*

Alas! The love of women!

It is known to be a L O V E L Y

and F E A R F U L thing!

—*George Noel Gordon, Lord Byron*

You call it MADNESS,
but I call it LOVE.

—*Don Bvas*

We sat side by side in the morning light and looked out at the F U T U R E together.

—*Brian Andres*

Love is like an eternal

FLAME. Once it is lit,

it will continue to

BURN for all time.

—*Kamila*

The supreme H A P P I N E S S
of life is the conviction that we
are L O V E D .

—*Victor Hugo*

If you have it [charm], you don't need to have anything else, and if you don't have it, it doesn't much matter what else you have.

—*Sir James M. Barrie*

But did thee
F E E L the
earth move?

—*Ernest Hemingway*

Yet they that know all things but know

That all this life can give us is

A child's laughter, a woman's K I S S .

—*William Butler Yeats*

kiss me

Their lips drew near, and clung into a

KISS;

A long, long kiss, a kiss of youth and

LOVE...

—*George Noel Gordon, Lord Byron*

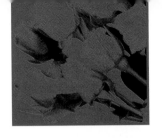

These two

Imparadis'd in

one another's

arms.

—John Milton

Amo, amas,

I love a lass,

As a cedar tall and slender;

Sweet cowslip's grace

Is her nominative case,

And she's of the feminine gender!

—*John O'Keefe*

Ah! When will this long weary day have end,

And lend me leave to come unto my love?

—*Edmund Spenser*

A kiss makes the HEART young again and wipes out the years.

—*Rupert Brooke*

BEAUTY is not in the face;

beauty is a light in

the HEART.

—*Kahlil Gibran*

LOVE builds
bridges where there
are none.

—*R.H. Delaney*

A kiss may not be the T R U T H,

but it is what we W I S H were true.

—*Steve Martin*

As P E R F U M E doth remain

in the folds where it hath lain,

So the thought of you, remaining

Deeply folded in my brain,

Will not leave me: all things leave me:

You R E M A I N.

—*Arthur Symons*

All thoughts,

all passions, all delights

Whatever stirs this mortal frame,

All are but ministers of Love,

And feed his S A C R E D flame.

—*Samuel Taylor Coleridge*

Come live with me, and be my love;

And we will all the pleasures prove

That valleys, groves, hills, and fields,

Woods or steepy mountain yields.

—*Christopher Marlowe*

For it was not into my ear
you whispered, but into
my H E A R T. It was
not my lips you kissed, but
my S O U L.

—*Judy Garland*

As he bent his head to come at her cheek she raised herself on tiptoe, and more by luck than good management T O U C H E D his lips with her own.

—*Colleen McCullough*

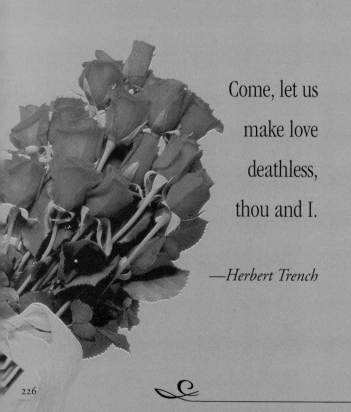

Come, let us

make love

deathless,

thou and I.

—*Herbert Trench*

Doubt that the stars are fire;

Doubt that the sun doth move;

Doubt truth to be a liar;

But never doubt I LOVE.

—*William Shakespeare*

For those who L O V E ...

time is E T E R N I T Y ...

—*Henry Van Dyke*

You are my love, my life…

my W O R L D.

—*Michelle Lozada*

BELOVED, all that
is harsh and difficult I
want for myself, and all
that is GENTLE and
SWEET for thee.

—*San Juan de la Cruz*

kiss me

Without L O V E, the world itself would not S U R V I V E.

—*Lope de Vega*

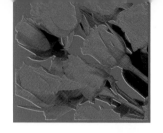

The sweetest hours

that e'er I spend

Are spent among

the lasses, O.

—*Robert Burns*

If you press me to say why I
L O V E D him, I can say no
more than it was because he was he
and I was I.

—*Michel Eyquem de Montaigne*

Kill then, and B L I S S me,

But first come K I S S me.

—*From* Thomas Morley

TOUCH is

the meaning of

being human.

—*Andrea Dworkin*

A continual atmosphere of hectic

P A S S I O N is very trying if

you haven't got any of

your own.

—*Dorothy L. Sayers*

It's not the men
in my L I F E
that counts—it's
the life in my
M E N.

—*Mae West*

kiss

The doctor must have put
[my pacemaker] in wrong. Every
time my husband K I S S E S me,
the garage door goes up.

—*Minnie Pearl*

For God's sake hold your tongue and

LET ME LOVE.

—*John Donne*

Wild Nights! Wild Nights! were I with thee

—Wild Nights would be our luxury—

Futile the winds to a heart in port,

Gone with the compass—Gone with the

chart—Rowing in Eden...Ah the Sea!

Might I but moor—Tonight in thee.

—Emily Dickinson

The ULTIMATE
experience of love is a
realization that beneath
the ILLUSION of
two-ness dwells identity:
"Each is both."

—*Joseph Campbell*

C'mon, baby, light my fire

Try to set the night on fire.

—*Jim Morrison and Robby Krieger*

I'll smother thee with K I S S E S ...

Ten kisses short as one, one long as twenty.

—*William Shakespeare*

First, to be able to

LOVE, then

to learn that

body and

SPIRIT

are one.

—*Hugo von Hofmannsthal*

The preservation of the species was a point of such necessity that Nature has secured it at all hazards by immensely overloading the passion, at the risk of perpetual crime and disorder.

—*Ralph Waldo Emerson*

LOVE reckons hours for
months, and days for years;
And every little absence is an age.

—*John Dryden*

LOVE one another, but make not a bond of love: let it rather be a moving sea between the shores of your souls.

—*Kahlil Gibran*

How do I L O V E thee?

Let me count the ways.

I love thee to the depth and

breadth and height

my soul can reach.

—*Elizabeth Barrett Browning*

He glared at her a moment through the dusk, and the next instant she felt his arms about her and his lips on her own lips. His K I S S was like white lightning, a flash that spread, and spread again, and stayed.

—*Henry James*

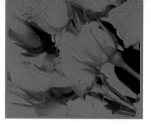

Absence is to

L O V E what

wind is to fire;

It extinguishes the

small, it kindles

the G R E A T .

—*Bussy-Rabutin*

258

N I G H T and day
you are the one,
Only you beneath the moon
and under the S U N .

—*Cole Porter*

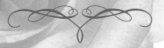

He that can jest at love has never loved.

—*Johann Caspar Lavater*

Our State cannot be
severed, we are one,
One Flesh; to lose thee
were to lose my self.

—John Milton

The minister kiss'd the fiddler's wife,

An' could na preach for thinkin' o't.

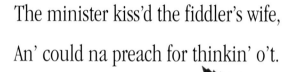

—*Robert Burns*

In L O V E , one
and one are one.

—*Jean-Paul Sartre*

kiss

The fickleness of the women whom I love is only equaled by the infernal constancy of the women who love me.

—*George Bernard Shaw*

My FIRST KISS can be summed up in one word: UNSUCCESSFUL.

—*Huey Lewis*

I met in the street a very poor young man who was in L O V E. His hat was old, his coat was threadbare—there were holes at his elbows; the water passed through his shoes and the stars through his S O U L.

—*Victor Hugo*

My bounty is as boundless as the sea,

My love as deep; the more I give to thee,

The more I have, for both are infinite.

—William Shakespeare

Mutual L O V E, the

Crown of all our B L I S S.

—*John Milton*

We are most

ALIVE when

we're in love.

—*John Updike*

Many an evening by the waters
did we watch the stately ships,
And our spirits rush'd together
at the TOUCHING of
the lips.

—*Alfred, Lord Tennyson*

A thing of no use, but
prized by two.

—*Robert Zwickey*

It is impossible to love

and be wise.

—*Francis Bacon*

Oh fie, miss, you
must not K I S S
and tell.

—*William Congreve*

I love your hills, and I love your dales,

And I love your flocks a-bleating—

But O, on the heather to lie together,

With both our H E A R T S a-beating!

—John Keats

kiss me

It was thy K I S S, Love, that
made me I M M O R T A L.

—*Margaret Witter Fuller*

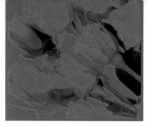

Let your L O V E
be like the misty
rain, coming
softly, but flooding
the river.

—*Madagascan saying*

[Being in love] is something like poetry. Certainly, you can analyze it and expound its various senses and intentions, but there is always something left over, mysteriously hovering between music and meaning.

—*Muriel Spark*

'Tis better to have L O V E D and lost

Than never to have L O V E D at all.

—Alfred, Lord Tennyson

One H E A T, all know, doth

drive out another,

One P A S S I O N doth expel

another still.

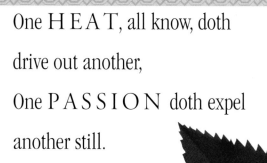

—*George Chapman*

If our PASSIONS are
aroused, we are apt to see
things in an exaggerated
way, or imagine what
does not exist.

—*Arthur Schopenhauer*

To a woman the FIRST KISS
is the end of the beginning; to a man
it is the beginning of the end.

—*Helen Rowland*

Some fine night the doors will open, and there I'll be…I hope before long to crush you with A MILLION KISSES burning as though beneath the equator.

—*Napoleon Bonaparte*

I am little other than a cloud at such seasons [of gloom]; but she contrives to make me a sunny one; for she gets into the remotest recesses of my H E A R T , and shines all through me.

—*Nathaniel Hawthorne*

PASSION often makes fools
of the wisest men and gives [to]
the silliest wisdom.

—François, Duc de La Rochefoucauld

I don't like F O N D.

It sounds like something

you would tell a dog.

Give me L O V E,

or nothing.

—*Alice Walker*

A kiss is a lovely T R I C K designed by nature to stop speech when words become superfluous.

—*Ingrid Bergman*

It was

ROSES,

ROSES,

all the way.

—*Robert Browning*

For thy sweet love remembered
such wealth brings
That then I scorn to change my
state with kings'.

—*William Shakespeare*

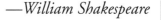

If thou must love me, let it be for naught
Except for love's sake only.

—Elizabeth Barrett Browning

If music be the food of love, play on,

Give me excess of it, that, surfeiting,

The appetite may sicken and so die.

—*William Shakespeare*

When S O U L

meets S O U L on

lovers' lips.

—*Percy Bysshe Shelley*

The Summer hath his joys,

And Winter his D E L I G H T S .

Though Love and all his

P L E A S U R E S are but toys,

They shorten tedious nights.

—Thomas Campion

kiss me

You were born TOGETHER, and
together you shall be forevermore…
But let there be spaces in your togetherness,
And let the winds of the HEAVENS
dance between you.

—*Kahlil Gibran*

L O V E , as everyone should know, is a strange disease.

—*W.C. Handy*

As a youth I had been woefully at fault, particularly in early adolescence. I had prayed to you for chastity and said, "Give me chastity and continence, but not yet."

—*St. Augustine*

Next to being married, a girl likes to be

crossed in L O V E a little now and then.

—*Jane Austen*

[He] would…K I S S me hard,

As if he plucked up kisses by the roots

That grew upon my lips.

—William Shakespeare

Like all the very young we took it
for granted that making love is child's
play.

—*Nancy Mitford*

LOVE rules

without rules.

—*Italian proverb*

kiss

A K I S S is strange. It's a living thing,
a communication, a whole wild emotion
expressed in a simple moist T O U C H .

—*Mickey Spillane*

What is a K I S S ? Why this, as some approve:

The sure, sweet cement, glue, and lime of love.

—*Robert Herrick*

I go where I LOVE and where I am loved.

—H.D. (Hilda Doolittle)

I'll come and make love to you at five o'clock. If I'm late start without me.

—*Tallulah Bankhead*

'Till I LOVED

I never lived—Enough.

—*Emily Dickinson*

A KISS is like

SINGING into

someone's mouth.

—*Diane Ackerman*

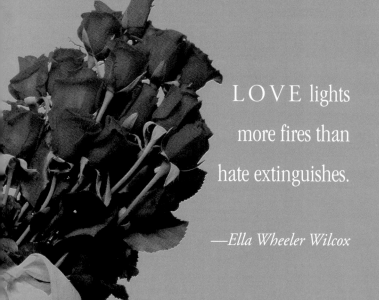

LOVE lights
more fires than
hate extinguishes.

—*Ella Wheeler Wilcox*

A GREAT LOVE is
an absolute isolation and an
absolute absorption.

—Ouida (Marie Louise de la Ramée)

All policy's allowed in
war and L O V E.

—Susannah Centlivre

I love you more

than my own skin.

—*Frida Kahlo*

LOVE was a great

disturbance.

—*Naomi Royde-Smith*

'Tis a S E C R E T

Told to the mouth

instead of to the ear.

—*Edmond Rostand*

kiss me

Lord, I wonder what F O O L it was
that first invented K I S S I N G !

—*Jonathan Swift*

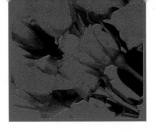

There is nothing
better for the spirit
or body than a love
affair. It elevates
thoughts and
flattens stomachs.

—Barbara Howar

330

Something made of nothing,

tasting very S W E E T,

A most delicious compound, with

ingredients C O M P L E T E.

—*Mary E. Buell*

You will know the R E A L meaning

of love when you F A L L in love.

—*A. Terance Dinesh*

It was first

LOVE.

There's no love

like that. I don't

wish it on a

SOUL.

—*Carol Matthau*

These impossible women! How they do get around us!

The poet was right: can't live with them, or without them!

—*Aristophanes*

A KISS is a
rosy dot placed on
the "i" in loving.

—*Edmond Rostand*

Whoso loves believes the

IMPOSSIBLE.

—*Elizabeth Barrett Browning*

The surest way of winning L O V E

is to look as if you didn't need it.

—*Ellen Glasgow*

Sex is one of the nine reasons for

reincarnation...

The other eight are unimportant.

—*Henry Miller*

The logic of

the H E A R T

is absurd.

—*Julie de Lespinasse*

My HEART is like a
SINGING bird.

—*Christina Rossetti*

343

All mankind L O V E a lover.

—*Ralph Waldo Emerson*

HARMONY is
pure love, for love is
complete agreement.

—*Lope de Vega*

There is only one happiness
in life, to love and
BE LOVED.

—*George Sand*

Because of

DEEP LOVE,

one is courageous.

—*Lao-Tzu*

Really, sex and laughter

do go very well together,

and I wondered—and

still do—which is the

more important.

—*Hermione Gingold*

kiss me

You can no more keep a martini in the refrigerator than you can keep a KISS there.

—*Bernard De Voto*

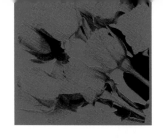

What is a kiss? Alacke! At worst,

A single Dropp to quenche a Thirst,

Tho' oft it prooves, in happie Hour,

The first sweet Dropp of our long Showre.

—*Charles Godfrey Leland*

Once he drew

With one long kiss my whole soul through

My lips.

—*Alfred, Lord Tennyson*

Do anything, but
let it produce joy.

—*Henry Miller*

PROTECT me from

what I want.

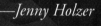

—*Jenny Holzer*

Love is a S P I R I T

of all compact of fire.

—*William Shakespeare*

kiss

LOVE ME

in full being.

—Elizabeth Barrett Browning

The great sea has set me in motion.

Set me A D R I F T,

And I move as a weed in the river.

The arch of S K Y

And mightiness of storms

E N C O M P A S S E S me,

And I am left

Trembling with J O Y.

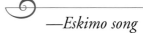

—Eskimo song

L I P S go dry and eyes grow wet

Waiting to be warmly met.

Keep them not in waiting yet;

K I S S E S kept are wasted.

—*Edmund Vance Cooke*

L O V E is a choice—not simply, or necessarily, a rational choice, but rather a willingness to be present to others without pretense or guile.

—Carter Heyward

Your words are my FOOD,

Your breath my WINE.

You are EVERYTHING to me.

—Sarah Bernhardt

The slowest K I S S makes
too much haste.

—*Thomas Middleton*

How absurd and

DELICIOUS

it is to be in love with

somebody younger than

yourself! Everybody

should try it.

—*Barbara Pym*

Nothing moves a W O M A N

so deeply as the boyhood of the

man she L O V E S .

–Annie Dillard

It requires infinitely a greater

genius to make L O V E,

than to make war.

–Ninon de L'Enclos

When L O V E
comes it comes
without effort, like
perfect weather.

—*Helen Yglesias*

And what do all the great words
come to in the end, but
that?—I love you—I am at rest
with you—I have come home.

—*Dorothy L. Sayers*

kiss me

Each kiss a heart-quake—for a kiss's
STRENGTH,
I think, it must be reckon'd by its
LENGTH.

—*George Noel Gordon, Lord Byron*

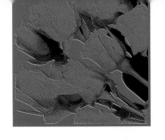

Free L O V E is

too expensive.

–*Bernadette Devlin*

378

LOVE has the quality of informing almost everything—even one's work.

–Sylvia Ashton-Warner

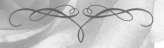

I don't know, it must have been the R O S E S, or the R I B B O N S in her long brown hair.

—*Robert Hunter*

The soul that can
speak with its eyes
can also K I S S
with a gaze.

—*Unknown*

kiss